DARK

Towards Light

DARK

Towards Light

A COLLECTION OF POEMS

Harsimran Kapoor

© 2024 Harsimran Kaur Kapoor

All rights reserved. No part of this book may be reproduced in any form or by any electronic or mechanical means, including information storage and retrieval systems, without permission in writing from the publisher, except by a reviewer, who may quote brief passages in a review.

ISBN: 978-1-0689298-0-9

First Edition

Cover design and Images by DALL.E

To the universe - I thank you!

This book is dedicated to my parents, with love. They first printed this book to show me it could be published.

I am immensely grateful to my aunts for reading this first draft and supporting it.

I wish my grandparents could've read it too.

Foreword

By Col. A.S. Kapoor: the Author's Father

From the earliest days, Harsimran's dreams and thoughts have found expression in her poetry. Her verses range from simple to complex, each reflecting her unique style and powerful yet subtle narration. As she steps into the literary world, I wish her the very best and look forward to seeing her touch the hearts of many with her words.

In the heart of darkness, there is light.

My twenties, a tumultuous decade at best, witnessed an insecure young woman grappling with a myriad of sporadic existential angst. I was unsure of what I felt, and why I felt it. And the only way to shake it off was to pen it down. When I revisited these poems at least a decade later, I saw a tapestry woven from the threads of introspection, memory, and the weave of my deeply human emotions. I am amazed by the power these words had to both heal and reveal.

Writing built me. It allowed me to bring my best self to the external world because my rhymes gave me an outlet for the worries of my inner world. The catharsis and creativity of writing these then, have allowed consistent reflection, pause and growth, to this day.

This book is my invitation to you to delve into the night and find your own stars. It is a call to embrace the darkness, not as an adversary, but as a canvas upon which the most authentic and luminescent parts of ourselves can be revealed.

A word, just a word
Yet, it's much more to me.
Mine, all mine
All I could imagine it to be.

I'm excited I get to share these poems of my youth with you. Thank you for reading this book. I appreciate you.

Parallel lines	1
Phoenix	4
The door	7
And it never happened	14
Purpose	16
The Unplanned Trip	20
Patience and silence	24
Love for sale	27
The job	31
Intimacy	34
Golden	36
Run	38
The peddler	41
Yet	43
Wish	45
Holding on to goodbye	47
You	49
It'll pass	51
The perfect catch	54
Burlesque	56
Whispers	59
Question	61
Unfinished	63
Dark, towards light	65

PARALLEL LINES

I once asked a boy to write a rhyme
about parallel lines.

I searched today in memory's maze,
In hidden nooks of yesterday.

Through corners of my mind, repaired,
For a verse that lived, I hoped, somewhere.

I searched my mail and conversations
and there it was: a *promise* of the rhyme.
My smile was bright, and it shined
But the rhyme itself I could not find.

What I found was a treasure trove
Years of banter, growth, and love.
Dialogues of everything and nothing,
Tales of life, honesty and some bluffing.

Of growing up and figuring out life.
Depth like this is now a thing of the past.
I found a young girl: defensive, rigid, innocent
Clung to beliefs she didn't quite grasp.

I found made-up phrases like 'Incredibad', 'time wounds all heels', and 'ignorance is a blister'
and rolled my eyes so far back that they are still stuck at the back of my head.
My heart is amused and grateful for this store of memories.
It's the best gossip novella of my life I read.

And how I read!

I read reams and reams of conversation
Till I found that instant when
Suspended in time

Hidden in a rhyme
I told *him*
We were parallel lines.

Side by side, but never to converge
We were parallel lines in this vast world.
So aligned, yet destined never to meet
It wasn't a circle we could complete.

An atmosphere, unfinished, had hung in the air,
"I'll write of it someday," he'd promised, unaware
that 'someday' was a ship that never docked,
In seas of time, it is eternally locked.

So, someday never came.

All I wanted to find was a simple rhyme
about parallel lines.
So I wrote it.

PHOENIX

When the last drop of wine is gone
and your last breath is in and out
when the air is clear and clean
and I lay bereft without

Dark

When the music stops
and the chatter on the box
won't fill the silence,
I reach out to you
and find me instead.

Phoenix, I see your flame
and I wait for your first breath.

You're whole again,
breaking down again.
In that crack of the cap
as it tears from the bottle,
at the ending life
of every drag
you turn to ashes
like my phoenix.
Then you rise
just to burn again.

When you are well and truly gone
I take a minute of silence
to respect your end
but there you are again.

I hold you dearly
for you are reborn
in my mind, in my heart.

Out of a golden box onto my hands,
Phoenix, I see your flame
rising above the shards of sand.

You're the promise of light
ready to go through the cycle of burning
as your life was meant to be.

In my hands, you're spent,
on my lips, you stay,
so close, yet so short-lived.

I reach out to you
and find me instead.
Phoenix, I see your flame
and I wait for your last breath.

I'll burn you to ashes again.

THE DOOR

Part 1

At fifteen, I closed a door.
Quietly, but firmly, nothing there to explore.
I turned my back, and let it fall from my gaze.
In one heartbeat, a decision was made.

At sixteen I added locks.
I reinforced the closure and removed the clock.
Padlocks and bolts sealed the frame.
I built a fortress, in solitude's name.

At seventeen, knob locks were popular.
I picked out a shade of green.
I stayed put, warm in my storm:
Untouchable, sheltered, pristine.

At eighteen, I threw away the key
Content in my self-capability.
I painted over the door, for good measure
That shade of purple was a pleasure.

And as the years passed
The door faded away from my recall.
I painted my inner room with so many colours
That door camouflaged into the wall.

Part 2

In my twenties, I added doors and windows
To my so far closed-off, cozy room.
I envisioned a life rich in layers
and found ways to let it bloom.

I added a "velux cabrio" for riches,
where I could let comfort in and let it stay
I carved out a door for friendships,

Etched each line with courage and a prayer.

I made a garage for the wheels to rest
while I did too, in between travels, blessed.
I added a garden of jade, red and yellow
for good health, wealth, old friends, and every new hello.

I built a study for wisdom and dreams,
Where ideas took flight, off of its picture window's seams.
I created a chamber for art, where creativity flowed,
The skylight made the hues change the colours, just so.

Part 3

Then as I turned into my third decade
I bumped my elbow hard and sharp.
The zing of pain shot up my arm
Piercing the very core of my heart.

I caught my breath and looked for the culprit
What had dared to pain me so?
I couldn't remember when last I was this brittle
And my eyes caught a knob in the wall,
a bit of green was up for show.

Ah, the door I closed at fifteen
A symbol of youthful days.
Now it was noted, and couldn't remain unseen
It was time to revisit that sealed way.

But how? The door was painted shut,
layers thick, a canvas of my years.
The green of seventeen peeked through:
a ghost of past fears.

I vaguely remembered locking it,
a young heart's naive quick,
And the key, oh the key!
Lost in time's fabric, thick

Part 4

In the rooms I built, I sought a sign,
For dreams or miracles in the corners of my mind.
Where, oh where, did that key go?
Lost in thoughts from long ago.

As I rummaged through memories too deep,
My hands worked, peeling layers steep.
Each coat of paint, a story untold,
Echoes of muses, both new and old.

Months passed, the lock came into view,
A vibrant patchwork, a spectrum of hue.
No key in hand, yet the truth was clear,
I remembered what the other side held, so far, so near.

Hesitant, yet yearning, I called to the past,
"Grant me the key, for I am ready at last."
And there, in the garden's embrace so mild,

I find the key, under a bushel going green to ripe.

I'd locked away joy and love's sweet embrace
I punished myself for another's disgrace.
Convinced I was, that it was my lone fight
Today I look back, and my heart is tight.

I remind myself of my rich life so far,
An abundant life, in all ways but one.
Nothing good happens fast, they say
With this key, I feel I've already won.

Part 5

Anticipation grips my soul, I pause.
I think back and recall vibrancy, laughter, and glee.
Behind these doors, where hopes of love did stroll,
I was happy, I was free.

I wash the dirt off and take in the key
My fingers run along its edges, its complex simplicity
I chuckle when in a drawer, I also find the clock
Leaving it there, I go to the door and turn the lock.

My smile wanes as I survey the scene,
Barren, lifeless land brooding in humid air,
Nothing here exudes joy or gleam,
What transpired in twenty years? I wonder in despair.

Stepping outside, I notice the fragile Banyan,
Once my refuge, now brittle and frail,
Not a soul in sight, where could they be?
Where has everyone set their sail?

Around the bend, I meet my younger self, so keen…
"You abandoned me here!" she accused with pain.
"I'm sorry," I whisper, guilt upon the scene,
"Where have they all gone?", my voice is faint.

"They moved on," she shared somberly,
"Many knocked on your door year after year,
But they all left, unable to still care,
Now no one remains to knock or cheer."

Except for you… me, I realize with dread.

Fifteen-year-old me and I swap stories.
She witnessed the lives of the people we had met.
They found happiness, I'm very glad
A life of love and shared experiences, a familial net.

I'm happy for their new lives, truly,
Yet puzzled by their collective retreat,
"Why did they leave and shun this land?
It could've thrived and been a vibrant street."

"Without your care, this place withered and declined,
Unable to sustain or provide for another,"

At my regret and grief, she says,
"Though those folks may never be back,
Perhaps new ones would stay if we tend it together."

I hug my younger self in thanks,
Our souls re-unite, and together we start,
Mending this side of the door, a small part at a time
Rebuilding this land, healing our heart.

AND IT NEVER HAPPENED

My pencil has an eraser at the end
It doesn't work very well
When I erase, the smudges expand
I see the evidence, still.

Dark

A trail of grey whispers.
Harsh shadows barely softened
Once so sharp, the story clear
Now in blots, it's lost in.

The heart of my pencil is a core too bold
Graphite dark as a stormy night
And I fear the non-erasure
Of this faux pas, bright as blight.

Perhaps, in the turn of a page
Lies a quiet burial of the past.
Perhaps, I can stick the sheets together
And keep the story away from minds, aghast

If prying eyes tried to part the sheets
The tale will forever be lost
And time will do to memory what it has always done
Delete the burden. Remove the cost.

I can still write.
Write. Erase. Hideaway. Destroy. Forget.
And it never happened.

PURPOSE

I went to meet an old, old woman
in a hut in a village in Tibet, where she lived.
I had travelled many a mile
for this visit, where the pathway finally led.

Dark

I had heard whispered stories about her
A God, she was.. or a Witch…
and I had built her up in my head
just as my left palm developed an itch.

I banged on the dilapidated door
with my twitchy left fist.
The evening star was on the horizon.
In floated the mist.

My legs ached from the uphill climb.
I longed for a cup of warm tea.
I shivered outside the woman's door
wondering if she'd be kind to me.

Not sure what I was expecting,
but this just wasn't it
The door opened and what greeted me
was a warm smile and the glow of a fireplace finely lit.

Old, but lively – she invited me in.
I accepted, mirroring that wrinkled smile.
She said she'd been expecting me,
that I had simply taken too much time to arrive.

I wasn't surprised, somehow
and that was the wonder.
It was humbling to realize
that I'd expected the magic of yonder.

Busying herself on the stove
"What do you seek, my child?"
Towering over her, feeling pretty useless
"Purpose" I replied.

She smiled a smile I couldn't fathom quite,
the glow of the fireplace was making my senses light.
The tea smelt heavenly; she poured me a cup
One sip was all it took; I gave my consciousness up.

I wasn't aware that I was asleep
till I awoke
The home, the tea, the lady
seemed all a dream or a joke…

Getting up from the bank of the river
I went down to the river bend
to wash up the dirt and the eerie feeling
that my search would never end.

Purpose, I had asked for
From that lady in the dream.
And then I saw her again
Collecting water from the stream…

I followed her like a mad person
Twigs and stones, broke my stride – making me fall.
For an old lady, she was quick
But surely deaf, as she did not heed my call.

When I finally caught up with her, she asked
"What do you seek, my child?",
Out of breath, and bruised, I replied
"Purpose."

She smiled that smile, now familiar to me
and gave me a pretty blue flower to see.
I took it, its beauty belied all
and as I took a whiff, I felt a fall.

I wasn't aware that I was asleep
till I awoke.
The river bend, the flower blue, the lady
seemed all a dream or a joke…

The subway train was where I waited
for my destination, so near, so away.
The employment section opened in my lap
unable to hold my attention for a second of the day.

What a weird dream, I wonder
as I get ready to disembark.
I catch a glimpse of an old, old Tibetan lady
and with that smile, she points at the station arch.

Too ridiculous, too much of a coincidence
I walk towards the station arch, spellbound.
Will this be it?
Will my purpose be finally found?

THE UNPLANNED TRIP

A little girl and her gramps
On a sunny Sunday, went downtown
For there was a mega circus in town
And she wanted to see the clown.

She skipped and asked him along the way
"What will he look like, Grandpa?"
The grandfather smiled and replied,
"Like a dream from afar."

The little girl was pensive
And thought about it for sometime
Her grandfather looked lovingly
At the angel of nine.

"I wish you could tell me more", she said,
"I don't understand."
"You'll have to wait and watch, my dear", he smiled
"The show will be really grand!!"

The circus tents stood grand and tall,
Laughter and cheers, the din was an enchanting call.
At her first glimpse of the clown, in colours so bright,
Red nose, white face, she jumped with absolute delight.

His bright red nose
Upon a chalk-white face
His colourful, frilly clothes
Made her stop in awe and gaze.

But in that crowd, there was a sudden stir,
A distant rumble began to occur.
Eyes widened, voices rose in fright,
A shadow fell, dimming the light.

It was then that the stampede began
The sunshine was drowned away
She reached out to her grandfather for protection
But she felt him being pulled away.

"Let me go to my grandpa please" she struggled
To unhearing ears, she pleaded and asked.
And when no one came to their rescue,
She did a holy task.

The fragile girl crawled to her grandpa,
But on a shove, he fell back.
She reached him in time and held him up
But strength, her small frame did lack.

Her grandpa, he slipped and fell
On top of her, unaware of where she stood.
In the blink of an eye, they were overrun
She, too, hit her head on the concrete and wood.

The last thing she heard
Were muffled shouts and cries for help.
She also heard herself yell.
Then darkness fell and silence dwelled.

When she opened her eyes,
It was a different sight.
Her grandfather was beside her
She was safe and it was unnaturally bright.

"Where are we Grandpa?, she threaded her small hand in his.
Is the clown somewhere near?
The grandfather looked at her gently
And blinked back the threatening tear.

"We are going to a place, my dear
Where children should seldom go."
"Oh! That sounds so exciting", she said
"Tell me more… hurry…Oh, Grandpa! You are so slow!!"

The grandfather's eyes stayed moist,
Because he could not explain
To his little princess,
the horrible, horrid pain.

"We won't be going home, my dear
In God's grace, we shall now stay"
Yes, it was an unplanned trip
And they had come too far away.

PATIENCE AND SILENCE

He approached a crossroad, a choice unseen
No one knew what he would glean
At the fork, he slowed his already languid pace
They watched; eyes peeled at the stoic face

Dark

They looked for a telltale sign
He looked fine. But he couldn't be... Could he?

He looked back, just once, a fleeting glance
Did he want to go back, they wondered, a second chance?
Do it all over again, this time differently?
Did the set of his jaw, or of his shoulders tell any story?

They searched for a shrug, a hint of pain,
For resignation's mark, tried too many times in vain.
They sought a tattletale in his calm facade,
But surely, he must be hiding a charade.

He turned his head, taking eons to decide,
His audience watched, their anticipation wide.
He didn't see them, but knew they were there,
Their silence loud, their supposed care laid bare

Their silence was loud as they waited
Their breath baited

He was at the fork of the road, resigned to his fate
Nothing more in this lifetime, nothing more than bait
He stepped to the left: a chance choice, led by his heart.
The last thing they saw as he took that fateful step
Were the first signs of emotion start
Shock, Awe – his eyes bright at what he beheld
Held away from their view by the angles

They craned their neck to see his sight
In vain, they were kept in the night
Instead, they watched him, gripping their seats tight,
This was the moment they'd left their warm hearths for, their delight

Even with emotion plain on his face,
They couldn't discern fear from elation's grace,
Anxiety from awe, they couldn't decode,
The price of silence, was weighed in gold.
There was only one rule to this game
Be patient; do not call out his name

A hundred thousand people had gathered to see
What this boy could finally be.
There was only one rule to follow
To alter their tomorrow
Yet, they could not see
Their hearts drummed at the anticipation
Sorrow or jubilation? End of tribulations?
Finally, will they know how it ends?
It had to end, didn't it?

Faint, barely audible… a whisper was heard by a few
"NO!"
A clang, a swoosh and the curtains came down
in a big, theatrical finale
The only rule had been broken

Patience and Silence.

LOVE FOR SALE

"Love is not for sale" Protests rang out: screams, shouts
"Love is not for sale" Everyone agreed without a doubt

But there was one to disagree,
a crooked smile wore he,
eyes cold and poised to make a decree

"I met God once", said he – in a low tone
"In a crowded place and no one saw.
I met God once…Was it faith or madness, I hardly know"

"God is just a boy", he drawled, "Hardly ten",
"Not a very interesting one either,
Despite all that he's been considered
since time knows when"

"When I met him, I was unaware
Who I had the fortune to meet
Or misfortune – I can't quite decide"
He shook his head, bemused, at the protest shouts
'Ignorance **isn't** bliss' on the street.

"He played with an unelaborate marble: green and blue", he continued
"And inside, he had what looked like toy soldiers, and toy maidens too."
"But when I saw closely, I saw a tiny doll like me and one that looked like you,
and this bartender, and yeah", he pointed lazily, "those two."

He studied his audience
They weren't buying the tale
They were protesting for love
Even stories here weren't for sale.

He grinned a grimace and continued
"I asked the boy about this trick and I looked closer

And as I did I saw my toy version also peering
into a smaller marble, green and blue with a lazy leisure."

"Magic man was He, I looked at him – ashen and pale
He laughed and predicted befittingly that no one would trust my tale"

"He said 'Yes, it is I who play this game!
All you know is but a mirage of my whim and use."
Distracted from fitting the marbles in weaves, he said
"I'm sorry to have barged in like this
But some of these puppet strings came loose."

The man with the crooked smile laughed
"To think about the years we've spent confused
As to why we're here, how to live
And ponder on all we have to lose"

The girl looked bored
"What's this story to do with the roars out there?"
She held up her hand "It's been a good story, mate
But what matters most today is if in a cause you care!"

The man with the grimace-like grin smiled.
"But there is a point to my tale.
The ten-year-old kid and I struck a bargain
Since I'd caught him merrily creating chaos and ail.

The boy offered to give me that for which I strive.
Freedom, hence I asked for life

But there was a price to pay even to the kid
He took something from me I never used yet always hid"

"God purchased any love and kindness I had in me
In return for the freedom I sought
It is quite amusing to see those others
Claiming love can't be bought."

"I don't ramble on without purpose.
There was a point to the tale.
As I parted ways with the boy
I heard God whisper to himself, amused
'Love has always been for sale'."

THE JOB

On days like these
The rain outside
Isn't as cold and clammy
As the moment in this room.

The chill seeps into the skin
Engulfs the bones
Makes them rigid.

The cold permeates the soul
Reaches the heart
Makes it crooked.

Sympathize, empathize
Yet stay indifferent.
Pass judgment on the failings of others.
Dismiss your role in this play.

It isn't your job to slay dragons.
They made their fate,
Don't waddle in that muddy water,
It'll make it harder for you to follow your dreams.

'I have a family, I have a kid
What will I tell them?'
'He has a family. He has a kid that calls him a hero.
What will he tell them?'

It is not your job. This is not a charity.
He'll have a better life out of this place. It isn't for him.
Pucker up the upper lip.
Your face reveals nothing.

State the facts.
Get a confession.

Document it.
Manage chaos and emotions.

The rain pelts outside.
Feel nothing.
Say nothing.
Give nothing away.

The heart is cold, now.
Hardened with time and practice.

He leaves.
Shoulders heavy with burdens
Of confessions, of failings
Of the vast unknown that awaits him.

Look on at that once proud gait
This today has lost to the battle
Of time, and numbers.

You did your job, You'll get your bonus.
So what if you died a bit today?

On days like these
The drizzle outside
Isn't as cold and clammy;

The cold outside
Is still warmer
Than you, as a person, would ever be.

INTIMACY

Closer are all of us, closer than we ever were
Where distance matters not
And histories are usually forgot
Friendships forged, attractions denied
Individualism celebrated, materialism eyed
You and I talk about everything

and it amounts to nothing at all.
We spend our time, swapping stories and dreams
Unrequited loves, open secrets and grandiose schemes.

Now virtual is as real as reality gets
And each of us laps up the fame that we beget.
Unknown, no longer – each a celebrity in their own right
Even though I know all about you, I've never held you in sight.

Effortlessly we stay in touch
And frankly, we know it doesn't amount to much.
Geographies are just lines on the ground
I can reach out to anyone, anytime, any way around.

All one has to do is choose from the 'available' list.
In case of a fallout, no one is ever truly missed.
You and I have much to say
We can spend talking all night and all day.

Do you see?
How we behave and what we do
With all the people we know:
Strangers, acquaintances, and friends, too

Do you see what I see?
How we waste time, effort, emotions and sanity
On conversations that are no longer a craved rarity
And all intelligence is sacrificed
Over pun plays and equivocality.

GOLDEN

Smitten, I lie
Intoxicated, obviated
You make happy be
I love everything about you
Your smell, your taste
Your strength in small quantities

Remarkable, reliable
You open my mind, numbing it to the world
Make me calm, take me high
Run to the clouds, daydream
Fall and run again

The room spins
And I'm feather-light
Transported to another world
As if on the whim of a breeze
The mix of power and humility
A prayer that'll bring me to my knees

Aware, I lie
In such clarity that would demand to be kept under wraps
But I peel it off
I like what I see

In my hand, the amber lies molten
Fire and ice… Promise and lies
Poison and medicine
I love how aptly it is golden.

RUN

The sweat drips from your temples; your insides burn
The rhythm of your footsteps
Whisper promises of distance
Your breath is ragged
Your throat parched
You have a sense of achievement

Dark

To have run from bereavement
The gravel at your feet
Is like white sand with black beads of memory
Trampling them, crushing them
You move with lithe grace

Away you move, towards something
Something you can almost reach
Almost touch, almost experience
A smoky thread of future beckons
and you run.

Your feet cripple and yet you don't stop
Your back is wet, your legs leaden
But you have a goal in sight
And you'll get there even if it takes all night

Things will look so different in the morning
You smile; you have a sense of achievement
To have run from bereavement
You laugh; another bout of energy
Courses through your body
Propelling you forward
Yes…almost there…It's almost light
You can almost see where you are now

Look around you, familiar visions
Your heart sinks; you've come a full circle
Or maybe you were never removed
From the scene from which you ran

Still here… Still here
But you won't accept it
This won't be the time you give up
You deny again
Close your eyes

Romance the darkness
and you run.

THE PEDDLER

Medicines…Medicines… Medication for sale
for every hurt, every scar, every ail.

Lonely? Try the social decree.
Blue? Go for a shopping spree.

Miss someone? Well, just move on.
Angry? Sleep on it and wait for dawn.

Medicines…Medicines… Medication for sale
will fill every hole in your soul, no matter the size or scale.

Bitter? Chocolate is the cure.
Suicidal? The promise of a better future - the lure.
Tired? Healthy eating is the key.
Jealous? Claw out all the competition you see.

Medicines…Medicines… Medication for sale
Try some. It has never failed.

Hurt? Cover it up and let it lie.
Scared? Unnoticed it goes under your 'me, myself and I'
Vulnerable? There is no room for that here
Giving up? You've been doing that from the start, my dear.

Medicines…Medicines… Medication for sale
for every hurt, every scar, every ail.

Medicines…Medicines… Medication for sale
will fill every hole in your soul, no matter the size or scale.

YET

Unknown, misidentified, misunderstood
Lay all my emotions, denied;
The longings, the want, the love, the hate
All transitioning into indifference and lies.

Yet, indifference wouldn't pain so much
If it were indeed just an outgrowth.
It wouldn't leave me disappointed in myself
Or in whomever for comfort I go.

Yet, comfort wouldn't distress me
If the dependency was identified and feared;
The knowledge that every embrace
In time, in cruelty would be seared.

Yet, cruelty would not ugly be
Bitter honesty is truthful still.
Yet truth is the hardest thing to face
the hardest hit, the coldest kill.

WISH

I wished tonight
that it hadn't rained that night
that you hadn't had that drink
that you hadn't ridden that bike.

I wished tonight
that I hear your voice when you'd call.
I wished not to miss you
or to have never met you at all.

I wished tonight
that I could rearrange the past, to rewind.
I wish you hadn't shown me you
No other as genuine, as kind.

I wished tonight
upon everything I could see or know
for different last words said so offhandedly,
for a chance for our story to unfold and grow.

I wished tonight
with regret, desperation and fear;
I wished a simple, impossible wish tonight
I wished you were here.

HOLDING ON TO GOODBYE

There is no substituting
your warm voice and touch
a whole life of weaving magic undone
in one cold whisper of wind, all of it ceased:

the retorts, the epigrams, the yarns
customized for each friend, those you loved dearly
whose eyes now spill shine,
like the diamonds you deserve.

The soft faces are pale
the long sighs are the songs you strummed,
the phone toyed with, willing for it to ring,
and your jokes over the phone, come to life
like my memories just now…
of all you were, all you promised to be,
taken in one swift act of indifference.

Who will do it again?
Mix friendship and love
in such a concoction that it is hard to identify if it were
fated or not, and hard to resist.

Who will do it again?
Take my hand and hold it tight
when in fear, or boredom, letting go is easier?

That's just it: no one.
And I can't do it either,
for anyone else but you.

I'm holding on to goodbye.

<u>YOU</u>

Here is the over-analysis of this
He reminds me of you
Intermittently, rarely
But in glimpses that I catch
Or those which catch me
He reminds me of you

Or maybe just of how it felt
Reciprocation: short-lived, as it may be
A universe apart, our timelines may be
Another life, another lifetime it may be
But in a turn of time, he reminds me of you

I loathe it and love it
Grateful that I still feel it
It's amusing how I'm running now
Chasing after shadows I thought I'd left behind
But they're still here aglow

It's a lost cause
He should let me go as he wants to
As you did, but maybe yours was a choice made for us

He reminds me of you
And of me
And I want to capture his worries and calm him down
As you did for me
Show him what it is to find peace
But I won't because I can't

Because still
He reminds me of you
Even when I don't want him to
He reminds me of you

He reminds me of you.

IT'LL PASS

Your piercing thoughts made you cut corners.
Your stabbing words led you to strife.
You like looking backward,
You love looking forward,
But being present?… suspends you in life

It'll pass.
Every love you've felt.
Every hurt you've had.
It'll pass.

You read suspense novels
because, with love stories, you can't relax.
Green with envy, you are, of fictional characters
They're bathed in abundance, yet, you're in lack.

It'll pass.
Every ache you've felt will dissolve into the flow.
It'll pass.
Watch the feeling be fleeting as it goes.

When the world is pretty, the sun shines bright,
And that's not in sync with the ice inside,
When the skies are blue, trees sprouting life,
And you're in your room hoping for rain…

Remember,
It'll pass.
It is just a turning tide.
It's the wave you need to ride,
Let it pass.

It'll pass.
So what if it takes a bit of you…
takes more than you have.

You're still here.
You're a shell now, nothing's left for fear.

It has passed.

THE PERFECT CATCH

They went out to wine and dine.
He charmed her with his flattery fine.
Pretty and carefree, seemingly shy, yet bold,
Her mind was on lavish gifts: clothes, bags, diamonds, gold.

The drinks were served, the oldest wine.
He went on to fake an enjoyment divine.
She had a glass, and another, a few.
Confessed with eyes downcast, this to her, was new.

Good food, fancy restaurants and shiny platters
She said she was uneducated in such matters.
So naïve, he thought in today's age and day.
Such a perfect candidate for an easy lay.

Victory, he thought, with half a smile.
Another feather in his cap, another walked a mile.
He ordered the high-priced number 68.
She said softly she could stay late.

So gullible, she thought, as she smiled at him.
Women can fleece any man at a whim.
A smile, a touch… one held gaze.
One sweet word can start a craze.

"I'll keep her around, till I find someone hot."
While her, "He'll do for a weekend's spot.

Games, oh games… Such a perfect match.
Neither ready to give and both set to snatch.

Soon enough, they'd scout for a fresher batch.
For now, each had their perfect catch.

BURLESQUE

It had been a long, strange time
We wandered along the stone-way path
My throat was parched
My legs, they ached
Beads of sweat, they lay on my neck
I longed to go back, to rest, to stay.

Not yet, whispered his excited voice
The tone of which was hoarse and tight
My legs moved on, the thirst denied
I wiped the moisture off my face
I must look the part, be strong yet meek
He egged me on, I followed him on that street

The road opened up, theatrically
Like a makeshift porch of green and grey
Dancers came pouring in as if, inadvertently
Twirling and shimmying
Elaborate, against a setting May

We sat on a boulder as they flocked our way
The dancers were provocative in the way they swayed

Did her scarf just fall?
Oh no! Oh yes!
Did that skirt just lift?
Oh no! Oh yes!

Not unlike their dance
Was the dance I danced
Their games rang true of the games I played
What they did with their clothes
I did with my eyes
My words, my smiles
To part, to stay

Did he just fall?
Oh yes! Oh no!
Would we have it all?
Oh yes! Oh no!

Was this dance so needed, so compelled?
Would I dance with him still if another fell?
Did he ever mean those words he said?
Or just for spectacle was my hand held?

Show and tell; yet, don't show much
Tickle the mind; ingrain a thought
I can play this game, frequently bought
I can provoke your attention and converse not

Do you prefer the meek?
Oh no! Oh yes!
You'd like me in glee?
Oh no! Oh yes!
Uncover, and then flee?
Oh no! Oh yes!
Who do you want me to be?

The show wound down and ours begun
Hand in hand we went ahead of the setting sun

The path downhill is easier now
Behind, the setting is picturesque
I now understand what he meant
When he said he loved burlesque.

WHISPERS

Be a writer, they whispered.
Regress into your comfort zone
And bleed on a piece of paper
Until the suspense is gone

Let the parchment soak in the bits of you
And let's let everyone see
Those words of depth only reveal
The shameful bits of me

Be a writer, they whispered
You have a way with words
Write the phrases
that no one's heard

Be a romantic, they whispered.
Dream of beauty and idealism
See the potential in each moment
Unmarred by realism

Deny the morons who scream
'You're a frog in the well, an innocent child'
Be a romantic, they whispered
You have an imagination wild

Be a poet, they whispered.
Go to dark places where weaknesses become a deluge
Extend a hand of your cultivation
Twist threads to make a threadbare refuge

It's a flimsy cover-up, but it'll do
Be a poet, they whispered

It's the gift of a few

QUESTION

If I cease to exist tomorrow,
I wonder what I would leave behind
Not a great friendship that stood the test of time
Not an honest, kind word that touched someone's life
Not experiences that float like balloons in the sky

Not many instances of genuine feeling: laughter, love, awe or joy,
Not anything at all to speak for my time here spent
If I cease to exist tomorrow, would I take time now to repent?

If I cease to exist tomorrow
There won't be much to say about how kind I was as a person or a friend
Because I wasn't much on any given day
I can just imagine the conversation among
The ones who'll show up, a few
"I just remember her by the things she used to do
The music, the writing and the rhymes"
And I wonder if I would change in time
If I'm not around tomorrow
Is it ok to be glad that everyone would be just fine?

If I cease to exist tomorrow
Would it matter… at all?
In a life of confusion, decisions, turmoil
Would I want to do more when it comes to the final call?

Not all of us give enough. Not all of us are 'good'
And while I know what I have done
When I go, will I leave a wake of coulds and shoulds?
The things I write out of habit to make sense of it all
These are the only things I'll have to show before my final fall

So, if I cease to exist tomorrow
Look back at my prose, stories and rhymes
When all is said and done, that's all I'll leave behind.

UNFINISHED

Stories of fiction and tales of fact
Disallowed thoughts about incomplete acts
From strokes of colour on canvases of white
To the whispers of the wind on the rides of my life

The sound of feet
Vibrating and playing in sound
The music I could have learned
Another bliss I could have found
For the things I could have done,
For the things, I can still do
For things that beckon still, not too late
I sit and list all the things I could have made:

Memories in a big bowl of timely experience
Visions to actions unhampered by conscience
Music to make you sigh
Song to help you describe
I could have made trouble
And enjoyed youthful haste
I could have taken chances in love
and given my rhymes a happy taste

I could have made time for a language
that'll drip from the mouth a bit wrong and misdone
I could've made a night of dancing
in the name of youth and, carefree fun
I could have made up stories that books would tell
Of angels, demons and mystic creatures
Of earth, of heaven, of hell

For, at the end of life, when I look back
I would see life's games I passionately played
And enjoy the completion of all the things
In this simple list, I made.

DARK, TOWARDS LIGHT

At dusk, I'd often sit to write,
Moved by feelings, which were seldom delight.
From bottled depths, my emotions sprung,
Through the pen, they found their tongue.

Once my words spilled into view,
I'd weave them fresh, a flow anew.
This act reframed my fleeting defeat,
Changing how the world I'd greet.

The darkness doesn't linger, it doesn't stay,
Once it's on paper, it softly drifts away.
And towards the light, I'm ever drawn,
I embrace the dark… and also the dawn.

Fin.

You've completed the night dive & enjoyed the bioluminescence!

ABOUT HARSIMRAN KAPOOR

I have always had a vivid imagination and a strong penchant for daydreams. While I have a day job that I enjoy, writing poetry comes naturally to me, much of it unintentionally, dark.

I was born and raised in India into a military family, so I've had the good fortune of living in many parts of the country. Today, I live and work in beautiful British Columbia, Canada enjoying the spectacular backdrop it provides to this phase of my life.

I've been writing since the age of eight. My first foray into poetry was a piece called "Sun," which was featured in my school magazine and recited by another student during a morning assembly.

This is my first publication. Thank you for picking it up.

www.ingramcontent.com/pod-product-compliance
Lightning Source LLC
LaVergne TN
LVHW041549070426
835507LV00011B/1008